THE CURIOUS

C000245426

"The brilliant and entertaining
a clear and enjoyable text tha
about the world and our place i,

LORD REES
Astronomer Royal, President of the Royal Society 2005–2010

"Too often science and faith are pitted against each other. This book
breaks down that split in a creative and engaging way. It shows the
scope of science in our lives and how the study of science and the study
of God feed and magnify each other. Human beings have always been
hungry for understanding and meaning, and this book beautifully
shows how this has worked out from the earliest time. It is a book
that leaves me in awe at the 'art' of science: for the way it unveils the
magnificence of God our Creator, who stretches out the canvas."

MOST REVEREND JUSTIN WELBY
Archbishop of Canterbury

"A witty and accessible treasure trove of scientific discoveries that
goes to the heart of our human quest to understand who we are.
This book doesn't dumb down or gloss over imponderables but will
leave you marvelling at the science and asking for more."

PROFESSOR REBECCA FITZGERALD
Director of Medical Studies, University of Cambridge
Lister Prize Fellowship (2008), NHS Innovation (2011), NIHR
Research Professorship (2013)

"Has the bug bitten you? Are you curious? Curious to know how
the universe evolved from the Big Bang? How matter arranges
itself into objects ranging from atomic nuclei to human beings,
planets,and stars? Are you curious to know why all these things are
the way they are?

Science is good for the 'how' questions but does not necessarily have the answers on the 'why' questions. Can science and religion talk to each other? Enjoy this series and learn more about science and the enriching dialogue between science and faith."

PROFESSOR ROLF HEUER
Director General of CERN from 2009 to 2015
President of the German Physical Society and President of the
SESAME Council

"Here is a wonderful and wittily written introduction to science as the art of asking open questions and not jumping to conclusions. It's also an amusing excursion through evolution and anthropology which packs in a lot of learning with the lightest of touches. A much-needed antidote to the bludgeoning crudity of so much writing in both science and religion."

REVEREND DOCTOR MALCOLM GUITE
Poet, singer-songwriter, priest, and academic
Chaplain at Girton College Cambridge

THE CURIOUS SCIENCE QUEST

HUNT WITH NEWTON

WHAT ARE THE SECRETS OF THE UNIVERSE?

To Lola

Best wishes

JULIA GOLDING

WITH ANDREW BRIGGS AND ROGER WAGNER

Roger Wagner *Andrew Briggs*

ILLUSTRATIONS BRETT HUDSON

LI🐾N
CHILDREN'S

Published by
Lion Hudson Limited
Wilkinson House, Jordan Hill Business Park,
Banbury Road, Oxford OX2 8DR, England
www.lionhudson.com

ISBN 978 0 7459 7753 9
e-ISBN 978 07459 7800 0

First edition 2018

Acknowledgments
This publication was made possible through the support of a grant from Templeton
Religion Trust. The opinions expressed in this publication are those of the authors and
do not necessarily reflect the views of Templeton Religion Trust.

A catalogue record for this book is available from the British Library

Printed and bound in the UK, September 2018, LH26

CONTENTS

INTRODUCTION

Life is full of big questions; what we might call *ultimate* questions. In the first three parts of *The Curious Science Quest* our intrepid time travellers, Harriet and Milton, explored three of the most important mysteries:

- When did humans start to ask questions?
- Who were the first scientists?
- What is our place in the universe?

They discovered that investigating our place in the world goes back far beyond recorded history. They then visited the people of Ancient Greece, who started asking big questions about the universe, such as "What came first?". The Greeks also asked more detailed questions about how things work, and thus invented science!

Harriet and Milton's next stop was the Islamic Golden Age, and then they dropped in on some medieval thinkers in Europe, ending up in the sixteenth and early seventeenth centuries (the Renaissance). They saw how a more accurate picture of our place in the universe was discovered, largely thanks to three investigators: Copernicus, Kepler, and Galileo.

But our travellers were left with many new questions. For example, how does the earth stay on its path around the sun? And what happens next for science? Milton and Harriet are on a quest to find out.

Our Time Travelling Guides

Meet our guides to the ultimate questions.

Harriet is a tortoise. She was collected by Charles Darwin on his famous voyage aboard The Beagle (1831–36), which was when he explored the world and saw many things that led him to the Theory of Evolution. Harriet was brought back in his suitcase to England to be the family pet. As a tortoise she can live for a very long time and is well over a hundred.

Harriet

Milton is a cat. He belongs to the famous twentieth-century physicist, Erwin Schrödinger, and inspired some of his owner's best ideas. Milton is not very good at making up his mind.

Milton

Curious Quest

Having noticed some curious words over the entrance to a famous laboratory in Cambridge University, Harriet and Milton decided to go on a quest to find out the answers to as many ultimate questions as they could. In fact, they agreed to travel in time to see all the important events in the history of science.

The works of the Lord are great,
sought out of all them that have pleasure therein

In this series, you are invited to go with them. But look out for the Curiosity Bug hidden in some intriguing places. See how many of these you can count. Answer on page 110.

We join them now as they head forward in time for their next adventure. Where will they start? Up a mountain, of course!

The Curiosity Bug

GOING TO THE TOP

"We're here!" Harriet switches off the time machine's uncertainty drive and their journey through the centuries slows, then stops.

Milton looks out of the time machine's window but all he can see are clouds.

"Harriet, don't open the door. I think we're still flying."

Harriet nudges a dial to turn up the heater. She feels the cold in her old age. "We're not. We've landed."

"But we're in the clouds."

"Can you think of another reason why that might be?" She takes her knitting out from her shell and begins a new row. Milton takes this as a sign that they won't be going anywhere for a while.

"Um, because it's foggy?"

"Good. But that's not the reason."

Milton screws up his whiskers. "Because... because we've landed on the back of a jumbo jet?"

"You're thinking along the right lines. But there are no planes in the seventeenth century."

"We're on a flying carpet?"

Harriet rolls her eyes. "Now you're getting much colder. Think big. And stationary."

Milton rolls over and stretches, rejecting the idea of an elephant standing still. "I know! We're on a mountain!"

"Yes. The Puy de Dôme, to give it a name. That's a mountain in the middle of France. I've made an appointment with someone so we can see the next big step in science. Hopefully the clouds will have lifted by the time she arrives."

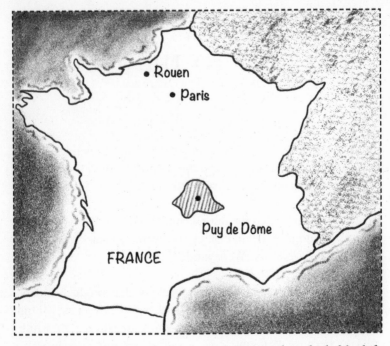

Milton plays with the ball of wool Harriet has foolishly left dangling outside her shell.

"Milton!" warns Harriet.

"I'm bored," he admits. "Is there always a lot of waiting around for this science stuff to happen?"

"How can you be bored when we're discovering the secrets of the universe?"

"I just want to discover them a bit quicker," he grumbles.

Harriet smiles. "People tried that. They leapt to conclusions without testing their ideas. Do you want me to tell you about one of them to pass the time? He's a hero of mine because he was so brilliantly wrong, yet also oddly right."

Milton rolls onto his front. "OK, then. Sock it to me."

"How did you know I was knitting a sock?"

Harriet's tale of Giambattista della Porta

"There once was an Italian thinker called Giambattista della Porta. He was born in 1535 and grew up in love with the idea of investigating nature. At that time, this meant he studied subjects *we* would recognize, such as mathematics and philosophy..."

"I like maths," says Milton, licking his paw. "I'm getting quite good at it."

Harriet gives him a hard stare.

"All right, I won't interrupt again. Carry on with your story."

"... *Philosophy*. But he also dabbled in astrology – that's telling fortunes by studying the stars. He also liked magic."

Milton jumps up excitedly, sparks of static electricity crackling out from his fur. "Oh, meow! Magic! Did he have a wand and go to magic school?"

Harriet sighs. "If such things really existed, I'm sure he would have been first in the queue. The point I'm trying to make, Milton, is that, like many people at the time, he didn't see a difference between science and magic.

"Giambattista's dad had big plans for his three sons. He wanted them to be gentlemen, so he sent them to a famous music school to learn gentlemanly arts – even though they had no musical talent whatsoever!

Boys, I think your talents might lie outside the musical scale, like your singing.

"On leaving school, Giambattista began to write on scientific subjects and turned out to be a wonderful cryptographer."

Milton snags the wool again without Harriet noticing. "What's a cryptographer?"

"Someone who can pass secret messages."

"Cool! How did he do it?"

"With eggs. He had a friend in prison, and he noticed that the insides of eggs were the only things that were allowed without being inspected."

"Of course you can't check inside an egg! But you can't write messages inside one, either. Not without breaking it," says Milton.

"Oh, really?"

GIAMBATTISTA SPY EGG INSTRUCTIONS

1. First take your egg.

2. Write your message on the shell with a mixture of plant pigments and alum (a chemical compound).

Secret Greetings from G

3. Now hard-boil your egg. The message will wash off, but not from the hardened white inside the shell.

4. Send to your friend in prison.

I cracked the message!

"That is so clever! Harriet, if ever you go to prison I promise I'll write you an egg," says Milton.

"Thanks – I think. Back to my story. Giambattista was the first person to question in print the old belief that garlic ruins magnets."

"Huh?"

"People had thought for centuries that if you rubbed a magnet with garlic it would stop working. It's likely that Giambattista got the idea this was false from an earlier scientist called Garzoni, but Garzoni's work could only be found in a manuscript locked away in a library, so few people knew about his discovery. Our lad went into print so everyone could read it. He described an experiment where he showed that the garlic hypothesis, or theory, was nonsense."

"So he's a real scientist, then, following the experimental method?"

"Yes – and no. He was very hit and miss with his ideas. For example, he also had another experiment where he claimed he saw scorpions being made from crushed basil."

"Oops," laughs Milton.

"I think his laboratory practices might have been a little lax." Harriet smiles. "He lived in Italy, where they have little scorpions running about in the wild."

"So what checks did he make to know which scorpions came along to investigate what he was doing and which came into being from his basil pile?"

"He oviously didn't."

"You can't make scorpions like that. He must've made it up." Milton rolls onto his back.

"Or he saw what he wanted to see. He was able to believe and disbelieve old ideas at the same time. He was like many thinkers of his era – a tangle of contradictions."

"Rather like your ball of wool," says Milton. He has made a mess of her yarn, playing cat's cradle with all four paws while she was caught up in the story.

"Milton!" says Harriet.

"I'll fix it, I promise. Go on about Giambattista. He was right on magnets, wrong on scorpions. Got it."

"Unfortunately, the church leaders sent over the Inquisition: a committee that looked into the views of believers. They weren't keen on Giambattista," continues Harriet.

"Why? He sounds like an entertaining guy."

"He was questioning what they thought were settled truths taught by ancient scientists, such as Aristotle. They didn't want that big picture to change."

"Not that old chestnut again! These Inquisition people have to move with the times!" says Milton, making a worse muddle of the wool in his attempt to untangle it. The time machine is also getting tied up and lets out a series of unhappy beeps.

"We're still in the sixteenth century. The big change comes in the next century. Poor old Giambattista was stopped from publishing, and his little group of friends in a club called the Men of Leisure was disbanded. He died in 1615, known to many as the Professor of Secrets. The end."

Milton sits on the mess, hoping Harriet won't notice. "But it wasn't the end for science, was it?"

"Absolutely not!" exclaims Harriet. "The beginning of another beginning, maybe. Look, here's a timeline for this part of our adventure. Have a quick look so you can get an idea of where we'll be going."

"Will there be snacks?" asks Milton, taking the list.

A Scientific Revolution: Harriet's Timeline of the Seventeenth and Eighteenth Centuries

Seventeenth century

1662 Robert Boyle devises Boyle's law of ideal gas

1665 *Philosophical Transactions of the Royal Society* published: the first journal with scientific articles checked out by fellow experts in the field

1628 William Harvey describes his discovery of the blood circulation system

1638 Galileo Galilei publishes laws of falling bodies

1643 Evangelista Torricelli invents the mercury barometer

1665 Robert Hooke discovers the cell

1675 Gottfried Leibniz and Newton both come up with an important mathematical method, now called calculus

1676 Ole Rømer gives first measurement of the speed of light

1674 Anton van Leeuwenhoek observes microorganisms by microscope

1687 Newton stuns the world with a classical mathematical description of universal gravitation and the three physical laws of motion

1672 Sir Isaac Newton announces that white light is a mixture of distinct colour rays

Eighteenth century

1745 Ewald Georg von Kleist creates first capacitor, the Leyden jar, important to the understanding of electricity

1752 Benjamin Franklin comes up with an experiment to prove that lightning is electrical

1763 Thomas Bayes publishes the first version of his theorem. This paved the way for Bayesian probability, used in modern machine learning, such as deciding whether an email is spam

1750 Joseph Black describes latent heat

1771 Charles Messier publishes catalogue of astronomical objects (Messier objects), now known to include galaxies, star clusters, and nebulae

1761 Mikhail Lomonosov discovers the atmosphere of Venus

1781 William Herschel, working with his sister Caroline, announces the discovery of Uranus, expanding the known boundaries of the solar system for the first time in modern history

1796 Edward Jenner makes advances in smallpox treatment through inoculation

1800 Alessandro Volta discovers the electrochemical series and invents the battery

1789 Antoine Lavoisier states the law of conservation of mass – the basis for chemistry, and the beginning of modern chemistry

1800 William Herschel discovers infrared radiation

1778 Antoine Lavoisier and Joseph Priestley discover oxygen

1796 Georges Cuvier establishes extinction as a fact

"That's a lot of advances!" says Milton.

"And where we're going we'll need some warm socks. We are going to be outside a lot." Harriet starts on a new row of knitting.

There is a scratch on the door of the time machine, saving Milton from having to confess about the wool.

"And I believe one of the next big moments is about to happen right now." Harriet goes to the door. "It's 1648, by the way."

Harriet opens the door and a big dog pushes its head into the gap. Milton's fur bristles so he looks like a toilet brush.

"Harriet, you did not say you had invited a dog to meet us!" he hisses. "I'll give you another experiment with a reliable outcome: dogs plus cats equals big fight!"

"Milton, manners! Marie, this is my friend Milton."

Marie pants and licks Harriet's shell. "Woof!"

"Marie is a gun dog and belongs to the family of our next scientific explorer. Is he outside?"

Marie woofs and scampers away.

"Doesn't she speak?" asks Milton, stepping outside cautiously.

"Of course, but she's very excited. History is about to be made."

Milton steps out onto a cold mountaintop. The clouds are breaking up, giving him a glimpse of the magnificent countryside of the Auvergne in France. The conical shape of the summit provides him with a clue to the fact that they are at the summit of an extinct volcano. At least, he hopes it is extinct. With Harriet you can never be sure what surprises she might have in store.

A little group of men are climbing up to the top. One man is carrying a glass tube and a flask filled with a silvery liquid. Another carries a basin.

"That's my master's brother-in-law, Florin!" barks Marie.

"Why's he bringing that tube up here?" asks Milton, keeping his distance from the eager dog. Fortunately, Marie is too preoccupied running rings around the men to be interested in teasing a cat.

Harriet catches up with Milton. "Florin Périer has a very clever brother-in-law called Blaise Pascal – that's Marie's master. Blaise lives in another part of France, without high mountains, so he asked Florin to conduct the test for him. A couple of scientific thinkers elsewhere in Europe have already done experiments with tubes of water, red wine, and other liquids, showing that if you turn them upside down in a basin of the same substance the liquid won't pour out but will come to rest at a certain height, leaving a gap at the top. For water this is a ten-metre gap, but you

23

would find it tricky to carry a tube of that length up a mountain."

"True. But why come up a mountain at all?"

"Patience, Milton! I'm getting to that. One of Galileo's students, Evangelista Torricelli, had the idea of trying the test with a much denser liquid, mercury. When the tube was turned upside down in the basin, the column dropped to 760 millimetres (mm), still with the gap at the top. He invented what we now call a barometer. But the question was: why did the liquid stop at that point?" Harriet pokes Milton.

"You're asking me?"

"Yes. You're on a scientific quest, so why don't you come up with some ideas to explain it?"

Milton squashes down his panic at being put on the spot. He always hates being picked on for an answer at his School for Clever Cats. But this is Harriet asking, not his scary teacher, Mr Mangy Tom. "Maybe something is stopping the mercury from running out into the basin?"

"Good. Go on."

They watch as the men set up their equipment on a flat rock.

"Do they put a lid on it so the level of the liquid in the basin can't rise up?" guesses Milton.

"No, the basin is open to the air."

A stiff breeze ruffles Milton's fur, pushing it flat. "So… does the air act as a kind of lid, pushing down on the surface of the liquid?"

"Well guessed," encourages Harriet. "The experimenters discovered air pressure. We don't normally notice it, but air presses down on us all the time. The column in the tube shows the point at which the air pressure stops the fluid from pouring out of the tube."

Milton squints at the sky, trying to see the atmosphere pressing down on him.

"You won't be able to see it that way. The big step forward for science is that Pascal decided you could test if this idea is correct by taking the same experiment up a mountain, where the air pressure is lower."

"I understand that. I'm nearer the limit of the earth's atmosphere so there's less air balanced on my head up here." Milton wobbles like a person trying to keep a book on their head.

"That's one way of putting it. But you don't have to think about balancing it. It's just there, surrounding you. What do you think the experimenters will see if they are right?"

Milton makes himself think. "If air pressure is the culprit, then the column of mercury shouldn't rise as far as it does at ground level."

"Great, Milton! You are really reasoning like a scientist!"

Suddenly the men start cheering and applauding. Marie gambols around them, then races over to Harriet and Milton.

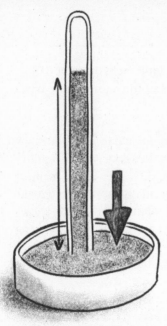

"Bow-wow! The column of mercury was 711mm high down in the valley. Up here it's 627mm! We're going down to check the valley measurement again, but I'd say that was excellent proof."

The men begin arguing as they pack up their kit.

"What are they talking about now?" asks Milton. "It looks quite heated."

"They're arguing about the gap at the top of the tube." Marie's tail is wagging so hard it is going in circles. "Some think it is a vacuum, but others are with Aristotle and say that vacuums can't exist in nature. They think there is kind of invisible vapour holding up the column."

"What do you think, Marie?" asks Harriet.

"I think that's enough experiments for today. I've been promised a meaty bone by my master. Au revoir!" She bounds off.

Milton is surprised to find he agrees with a dog, of all creatures. "Time for lunch, Harriet?"

"All right. But we're on a tight schedule. There is so much to see."

Milton preens his whiskers. "We're in a time machine, my friend. We can arrive whenever we want."

Harriet stops on the threshold of the box. "You're right, Milton. I'm getting carried away with excitement, like Marie."

"She certainly is eager," Milton says, watching the dog, who is already halfway down to the valley. "And not so bad for a dog."

"Then let's take a break for a double lettuce sandwich for me, and fish fingers for you, to celebrate the success of the barometer experiment."

TRY THIS AT HOME: BUILD YOUR OWN BAROMETER

There are a few steps to this experiment, but if you follow them correctly, you will have built your very own barometer, just like Marie's master.

You will need:

- A jam jar with a wide opening
- A balloon (do not use one that has already been blown up)
- A few rubber bands
- A tube of craft glue
- Sticky tape
- 2 plastic drinking straws
- A small piece of brightly coloured thick paper
- A ruler
- A pair of scissors

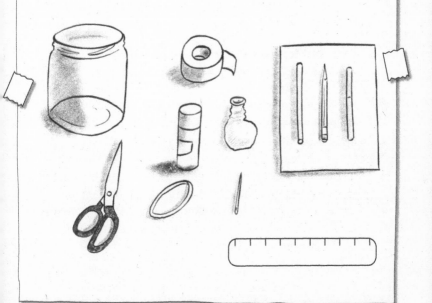

1. Set the jar on a straight, firm surface.

2. Cut the balloon so you have a nice round part left, without the long end.

3. Stretch the balloon so it fits over the mouth of the jar nice and tightly – the tighter the better.

4. Use the rubber bands to keep the balloon firmly in place over the mouth of the jar. We don't want any leaks!

5. Cut out the shape of a small arrowhead from the card. Tape the arrowhead to one end of the straw.

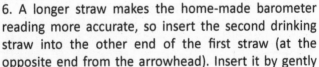

6. A longer straw makes the home-made barometer reading more accurate, so insert the second drinking straw into the other end of the first straw (at the opposite end from the arrowhead). Insert it by gently squeezing the tip of the straw and then push it in just a little bit so they become a long, yet stable, straw.

7. Drip a bit of craft glue onto the balloon covering, in the very middle. Place the empty end of the long plastic drinking straw on the glue. Gently secure it in place with light pressure and then tape it down until the glue dries and holds the straw in place.

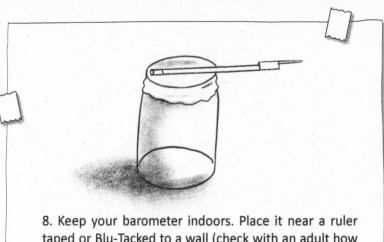

8. Keep your barometer indoors. Place it near a ruler taped or Blu-Tacked to a wall (check with an adult how best to do this). Arrange the arrowhead so that it points to the ruler markings. Watch your straw arrowhead over several days and record what you see in a weather journal. Do a few readings each day at the same time of day so you can compare the changes more accurately.

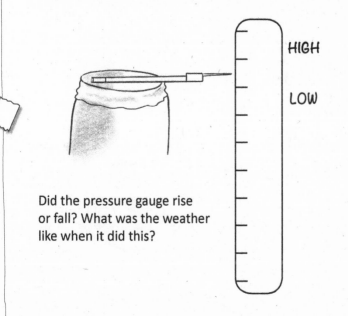

HIGH

LOW

Did the pressure gauge rise or fall? What was the weather like when it did this?

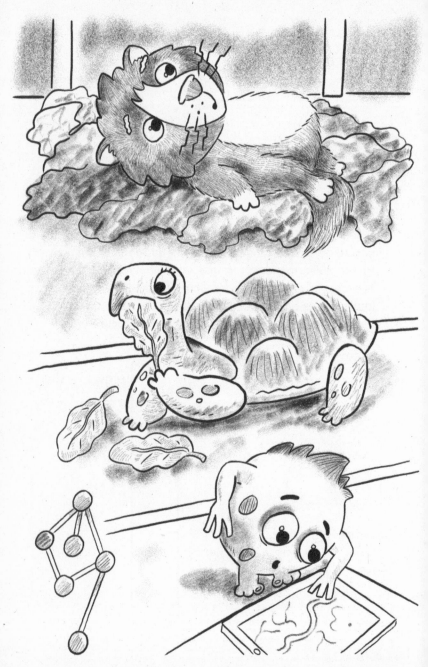

LONDON DAZZLERS

Harriet set the time machine in a gentle loop between the sixteenth and seventeenth centuries while they were eating their meal. Milton has polished off a big plate of fish fingers and is now grooming himself.

"So what big picture of the world do you think those French experimenters were showing us?" Harriet asks.

Milton has made himself comfortable on his new bed of tangled wool. He yawns, too lazy to think. "You tell me."

"I think they believe the universe can be understood. They think that it has secrets we can discover. Most of them believe there is an order to it, a God behind it, wanting us to ask these kinds of big questions."

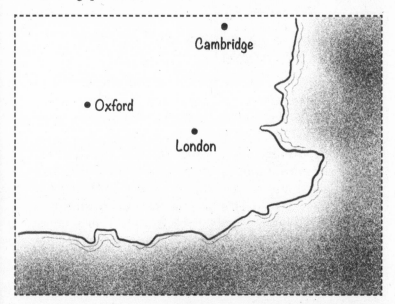

"Hmm." Milton is almost asleep.

"It doesn't have to be that way, Milton." She throws a lettuce stalk at him, but it bounces off his full tummy. "The universe could be random and meaningless, but some people investigated and found evidence that it has physical laws. That led many of them to form the big picture that there is an ordering presence behind it all; otherwise, why the patterns?" Harriet realizes she is losing him, and she doesn't feel like a nap just now. She wants to go on exploring. Things are just hotting up for science. "Milton?"

"Yes, Harriet."

"When's your birthday?"

An eye pops open. "Have you forgotten? It's next Tuesday – in our time."

"Do you think everyone knows when their birthday is?"

"Of course! It's one of the first things we learn because we get presents and cake and parties and…"

"I haven't forgotten your birthday," she promises. "But do you know that for most of human history people didn't know things like that?"

GREGORY'S CALENDAR: GIVE US BACK OUR ELEVEN DAYS!

Today we use the Gregorian calendar to measure the year. This is named after Pope Gregory XIII, who brought in the change in Catholic countries from the old Roman Julian calendar in October 1582.

Why change? Because the old system wasn't very accurate in measuring the length of the year. Faith leaders throughout history have often encouraged astronomers and others who are able to accurately work out the date because it helps organize the religious year – an example of science working well in the slipstream of religion! The Pope realized that Christian festivals were losing touch with their original position in the year, particularly Easter, which is calculated according to the date of the March equinox – which means when day and night are of equal length. The Gregorian calendar made a 0.002% correction. That, plus the adjustment introduced with leap years, means our calendar doesn't fall behind the passage of the earth around the sun.

Britain didn't catch up until 1752. The Act of Parliament that introduced the Gregorian calendar made two major changes. New Year used to fall on 25 March. It was moved to 1 January. This made 1751 a short year in official records (it only ran from March to December). It also skipped eleven days: Wednesday 2 September 1752 was followed by Thursday 14 September 1752. This led to the myth that there were riots and people demanding their eleven days back. Historians now say this is unlikely to be true, but if your birthday fell on one of those days you might well have been annoyed!

"So they really weren't sure when their birthday was? How sad!" says Milton.

"For example, no one is 100 per cent sure of Shakespeare's actual birthday. And even a royal person from the same time, such as Grand Duke Ferdinand of Tuscany, was a bit shaky on his date of birth when he asked Galileo to draw up his horoscope – a star chart for the day of his birth. Facts didn't exist."

"Don't be silly! Of course they did."

"No, they didn't. The word 'fact' didn't even exist. No one knew that they needed it."

Milton is awake now. "Harriet, this is blowing my mind. They had to know stuff, so what word did they use instead for things that were real?"

"Most relied on the authorities of the past for what they called their truths. That's why some of the ideas were so hard to dispel. There was an ancient idea, for example, that if you put a certain ointment on a blade it would cure the wound the sword inflicted. Someone had said it was true, and another person repeated what they said, and everyone went along with the idea that somewhere in the world this had been shown to work."

"That's stupid."

"To us. But at that time, how were they to know it wasn't true?" Harriet shrugs, bringing her shell up to her nose and down again.

"They should have tested it like Giambattista della Porta did with the garlic," he said.

"That's exactly what is happening out there," she says, waving toward the seventeenth century beyond the porthole. "The change in the big picture is from trust in old ideas about the secrets of the universe to a new picture where people find out for themselves. It was all helped by the printing press making the exchange of ideas much quicker. It takes weeks now, rather than years, for ideas to spread."

"I wonder what they'd make of the Internet."

"I think they would be flabbergasted."

"But we've seen people experimenting before: our friend Philoponus in Alexandria, and Roger Bacon Sandwich of Oxford."

"It's just Roger Bacon. Sandwiches hadn't been invented yet, but that's another story. You're right, though, there were some early pioneers, but their method becomes widespread at this point. It gradually came to be considered the only right way of doing science – and it still is. Milton, I've been waiting to say it, but we are finally here. Welcome to the dawn of the modern scientific age!"

Milton does a little dance on his woolly bed. "That sounds fun. Where are we going next?"

Harriet inputs a destination. "We're going clubbing."

Milton bounds over to the cupboard where he has stored his belongings. "I'd better get dressed then. I want to look like a cool cat if I'm meeting the 'in' crowd at the club."

"Um…" Harriet decides not to ruin the moment for him.

Milton comes back wearing shades and a bling collar.

"How do I look?"

"Very… um… fetching." She checks the dial. "And we are here. London's top nightspot."

They emerge among the moving legs of a group of gentlemen heading down an alleyway toward an open door. Light rain is falling and the air smells of smoke. Harriet shivers, glad she has remembered to put on her scarf and boots.

From inside the building they can hear the sound of laughter and conversation. Slipping in under the coat-tails of the last man they find themselves in a grand room with club-goers sitting around a huge polished table. Portraits of men wearing lace collars look down on gentlemen with long wigs.

Milton flicks off his shades. "Where's the music? The DJ? The dancing?"

"And the women members?" mutters Harriet. "Milton, welcome to a meeting of the Royal Society, London. It's 1665."

"So when you said 'club' you meant a place for people to hold meetings and exchange ideas, not to dance the night away?"

"I'm afraid so."

Milton shrugs off his sparkly collar with a sigh.

A hand reaches down and scoops him up off the floor. "What's this? A pretty kitty?"

Milton preens and finds himself nose to nose with a gentleman in a curly brown wig. The man settles Milton in his arms and strokes his back.

"I've found us a new member!" he declares to his colleagues. "Mr Cat, an expert in the art of rat-catching. I swear London is plagued by them at present, and we need him badly."

"Oh, do sit down, Pepys," says an angry-looking man who is already seated at the table. "Cats belong in the kitchen, not at society meetings."

"What's got your microscope in a twist, Hooke?" asks another. "We keep Pepys around for his conversation and clever remarks rather than for his information. You can't blame him for being amusing."

"I thought this was a club for men of science, not navy clerks, Wren," grumbles Hooke.

"I'm an architect. Are you going to show me the door too?" says Wren. "Best put the cat down on a chair, Pepys, and let Boyle begin his paper."

Milton slips out of Pepys's arms and down onto the floor. Harriet meets him under the table among a forest of polished shoes and boots.

"This is so exciting!" she whispers. "You've just met three of the most important people from this period. They all belong to the club! There's Samuel Pepys, who becomes world famous for his fascinating diary; Christopher Wren, a renowned architect who goes on to design St Paul's cathedral; and Robert Hooke, celebrated for his making of scientific instruments and studies of microorganisms."

"Micro what?"

"Little creatures you can only see with a microscope."

"And Hooke, I suppose, is the charming man who hates cats?"

"I'm afraid so. He isn't that keen on anyone or anything, so don't take it personally. If he were left on his own in a room he'd pick a fight with himself within five minutes."

The man seated at the head of the table begins to read out his paper.

"That's Robert Boyle, probably the most famous man in the room," Harriet whispers.

Milton finds his eyes closing in the warmth.

"Not again!" Harriet nudges him awake. "Look, we'll go and visit Boyle in his laboratory. You'll understand why he's so important when you see what he gets up to during his experiments. But for the moment I want you to remember that these men are all united in their search for that new thing: a fact. And their motto is: 'Take nobody's word for it.'"

"But you want me to take your word for it that that's their motto?" teases Milton.

"You can see for yourself. They've written it up in Latin over there."

NULLIUS IN VERBA

"Sounds like a spell. *Nullius in verba!*" Milton waves an imaginary wand. "Kapow!"

"It certainly helped transfigure science, so maybe it does have a little magic to it," agrees Harriet. "They changed knowledge from something you accepted into something you tested. Many of the original members first began meeting in Oxford during a time called the Civil War. That was a period when England got rid of the monarchy for a short while. They were known there as the Oxonian Sparkles. After Charles II was restored to the throne, some of them were forced to move.

"They went to London, where they found other clever thinkers. Together they formed the Royal Society and became what I call the London Dazzlers, because from being bright sparks they went on to dazzle the world.

"Suddenly, there were facts everywhere and the newly coined word was even written down in the society's founding document. But let's get back to the time machine and skip back a few years to Boyle's laboratory in Oxford."

Bringing science to the Boyle

Harriet lands the time machine in a herb garden. Milton can smell the scents as soon as the door is open.

"This is Deep Hall in 1661." Harriet steps out and nibbles on some mint. "In this year, Boyle publishes a book in which he says that his investigations are all to show the glory of the Author of them. He means God."

ROBERT BOYLE

- Lived: 1627–1691 AD
- Number of jobs: 5 (chemist, physicist, theologian, inventor, alchemist)
- Influence (out of 100): 92 (first modern chemist and discovered Boyle's law on gases)
- Right? (out of 20): 18 (in addition to discoveries, he contributes to establishing experimental method as standard for science)
- Helpfully wrong? (out of 10): 5 (as an alchemist he believed you could make gold from base metal. Seeking this helped develop apparatus for chemical experiments)
- Interesting fact: he lived in London from 1668 with his sister Katherine Jones. People at the time recognized that she was a partner in his work, but later she was written out of the account of his life.

"So he's one of the scientists who has a big picture that the laws of the universe point to a creator?" Milton has sniffed some catnip. Harriet has to hang on to his tail to stop him rolling in it.

"That's right. Milton, focus!"

Fortunately, they are both distracted by some odd noises coming from inside the house.

"What's he doing?" asks Milton, letting Harriet tow him away from the herbs.

"You remember that gap at the top of the mercury tube – the one the Frenchmen were arguing over?"

"Yes. They couldn't decide whether it was a vacuum or not." Milton pauses to scratch behind his ear. He's been very itchy since lurking in the alleyway outside the Royal Society. "What's a vacuum, by the way? You don't mean a vacuum cleaner, do you?"

Harriet smiles. "No, but I'm glad you asked. It's important to ask if you don't understand a word. A vacuum is a space empty of matter."

"Like my tummy when I'm hungry?"

"No, like outer space. Empty of everything, even air. Robert Boyle is intrigued by the gap and has come up with a way of investigating it. Let's go in and see."

Milton begins to follow her but jumps behind a rosemary bush as he spots someone at the door. "It's that man Hooke again! What's he doing here?"

"Hooke might have a difficult personality, but he really is the best instrument maker alive. He makes Boyle's experiments possible. We should go in and listen."

They creep into a dark corner of the laboratory.

"So, Mr Boyle, how are the tests progressing?" asks Hooke.

Boyle shakes his visitor's hand. "Excellently, Hooke. Thanks to your contraption that removes air from this glass bulb I have discovered that sound does not travel in a vacuum."

Hooke moves closer. He is very short, so he has to stand on a stool to see inside the glass bulb. "Fascinating. How did you find that out?"

"I put a bell inside, and when it was rung I couldn't hear a thing. Next I put a candle inside and the flame went out, so I deduced that a vacuum was missing something that fire needed to burn."

"Have you used the J-shaped tube I made you?"

"Indeed." Boyle holds up a tube shaped like an upside-down walking stick. "I've also found that air has what I call a 'spring'. If you pour increasing amounts of mercury into this tube the air trapped at the end is put under more pressure as the space decreases. I think I can show that mathematically. Have a look at this."

"What does it say?"

"If you multiply the pressure of the gas (P) by its volume (V), the answer is a constant, which I call 'k'."

"Milton, you're the one who's good at mathematics," whispers Harriet. "Do you understand him?"

"I think I do," purrs Milton. "Imagine my birthday party..."

She rolls her eyes. "I haven't forgotten, I promise."

"Imagine balloons..."

"All right."

"I have a small one and a big one, but have put the same amount of air in each. If you take a measurement and multiply the pressure of the air in each balloon by the volume of the balloon you come up with the same answer. That, in turn, means there is a relationship between air pressure and volume. They are connected by a law, not random results."

"So in that test there is more pressure in the small balloon and it might go pop, while the big one is flabby and not so good to play with."

"That is the side effect," agrees Milton. "Remember to blow the balloons for my party up properly."

TRY THIS AT HOME:

TESTING BOYLE'S LAW - "GAS PRESSURE INCREASES, VOLUME DECREASES"

Want to see Boyle's law in action for yourself? For this experiment you will need a balloon and a 50 ml syringe with a plunger (the kind that measures out liquid – not one with a sharp point!). Best to ask an adult to find you one.

You will need:
- A syringe
- A balloon (do not use one that has already been blown up)

1. Blow a little air into the balloon so it isn't completely flat, then pop it inside the syringe. Now replace the plunger. If you move the plunger with the outlet (syringe tip) open, the balloon won't change shape. Now try this with the outlet covered. What do you see?

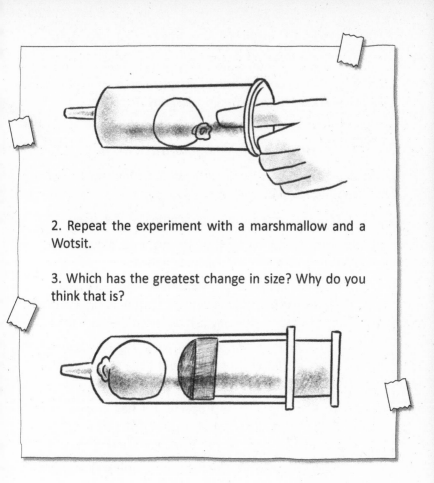

2. Repeat the experiment with a marshmallow and a Wotsit.

3. Which has the greatest change in size? Why do you think that is?

"Ah! We have a curious visitor!" exclaims Boyle. He picks Harriet up. "A tortoise. It must have become very lost to be here."

"It looks like someone's pet," observes Hooke. "It's wearing a scarf."

Boyle looks between his glass bulb and Harriet. "What would happen, do you think, if we put it in there? Would it be able to survive in a vacuum?"

Milton jumps out of his corner, hissing and spitting.

"Just a thought experiment, my dear cat." Boyle puts Harriet down. "I must ask the warden of the college if anyone has lost an exotic pet recently. Run along – you have a reprieve."

"That's not like you, Boyle. You usually prefer to do your experiments for real rather than puzzle them out in your head." Hooke peers at Harriet through a magnifying glass.

Harriet's Experimental Method

An experiment is an investigation to test an idea or hypothesis scientifically. It has six steps.

1. Make an observation, e.g. Milton likes fish fingers.

2. Form an idea as to why that might be: a hypothesis, e.g. all cats prefer fish fingers to lettuce.

3. Conduct an experiment with controlled conditions. In this case, gather a sample group of cats (e.g. 10) and put them in a room with only fish fingers and lettuce to eat.

4. Carefully note the results. There might be one cat that prefers lettuce, so you might have to adjust your thinking.

5. Look at the data and decide if it has proved your hypothesis. In this example you might conclude that "nine out of ten cats prefer fish fingers to lettuce".

6. Publish your results so that other scientists can check and correct your work by repeating the experiment.

Signed

Harriet the Tortoise

"And so I do," replies Boyle. "Experiments are the key to good scientific practice. When someone challenges my ideas I take it as a sign that I must provide more proof. So if I want to show that my theory about life not surviving in a vacuum is correct I must think up a clever way of demonstrating this – and from those results go on to come up with my fact. And until I know why the vacuum doesn't support life I must keep my ideas separate from the results. Jumbling them up confuses what we know with what we think might be so."

BOYLE AND FRIENDS VS THE ANCIENTS

Boyle and his colleagues, including Walter Charleton, were among the first to take on some old ideas and prove experimentally that they were completely cuckoo.

Contrary to what they said, goat's blood does not soften diamonds!

Milton is having a good scratch over by the fireplace. Hooke picks him up by the scruff of the neck. "Do you mind if I borrow this?"

Boyle is distracted by his next experiment and waves him away. "Go ahead. It's not mine."

"I want to look at something under my microscope, and I think he'll do nicely." Hooke tucks Milton inside his coat and hurries off, unaware that Harriet is tailing him.

"Milton!" cries Harriet. "You really must stop being so interesting to scientists! I'll save you!"

Harriet realizes it will take her half a day to follow the quick-walking Hooke, so gets back inside the time machine. She finds the device monitoring Milton's homing signal buried under a mound of wool. Pushing her yarn aside, she programs in the coordinates. In a flash, she lands a few streets away before Hooke has even arrived back at his laboratory with Milton. This gives her

a chance to hide under a pile of papers on his workbench.

"Stop squirming! I can't stand cats," mutters Hooke as he walks in. "They make me sneeze! But I need something and I think you have it."

He dumps Milton on the counter and picks up a magnifying glass. "Hold still!" Taking a pair of tweezers, he plucks something from Milton's neck. "I knew it! A flea!" He puts it on a glass slide. "There, you're free to go, cat."

Harriet beckons Milton over to her hiding place. Milton slinks over and joins her.

"He didn't hurt you, did he?" she whispers.

Milton rubs at his neck. "I don't like his manners, but I think he's done me a favour. I must have picked that flea up in London."

"We'll check there are no more when we get back in the machine. For now, we shouldn't miss this chance to see another scientific first."

"He invents something?"

"Oh, yes."

"What? A device to ruin everyone's day?" Milton smirks.

"No. He is one of the inventors of microbiology – that is, the study of very small living things. In fact, if you think about it, our not-a-people-person Hooke is partly responsible for saving many, many lives through later medical advances that use the tool he helped pioneer: the microscope."

"I'm not even sure that thought would make him happy!"

By now, Hooke has Milton's flea under his microscope. "Good gracious! What a monster!" He picks up a pen and starts to sketch. "You are a beauty, aren't you?"

"He sounds almost happy," whispers Milton.

"He is. He loves his work."

"I've seen such marvels through this device. You should see my drawing of a slice of cork," Hooke continues.

"Is he talking to us?" asks Milton.

"No, I think he's talking to the flea. He doesn't get out much."

"I'm calling the little structures I saw

'cells' as they remind me of the rooms monks live in. I wonder if it will catch on as a term. That would be pleasing – to have all those rich men using my ways of describing the fundamental building blocks of life!" He chuckles.

Harriet nudges Milton. "See, I think a lot of his anger comes from the fact that he's poorer than many of the people he meets at the Royal Society, and from a lower social background. He has a big chip on his shoulder that he has to struggle to do the same research when they have private fortunes to fund theirs."

Milton is beginning to feel a little sorry for Hooke. "He's also very short. He must get teased all the time."

"I'm afraid so. He is perhaps a little overlooked as a scientific genius."

Milton groans.

"Sorry, no pun intended. But we'll come to that later as this won't be our last meeting with the clever, difficult Mr Hooke. Time to go." Harriet climbs down off the table.

NEWTON'S CALCULATED INSULT

Isaac Newton is famous for his humble saying that he was only able to make his discoveries because he stood on "the shoulders of giants", meaning the scientists who came before him. That's very true for any person working in science. But there is more to it than that! The problem is that Newton's remark is in a letter to the famously short Hooke, with whom he frequently argued. So though he is congratulating Hooke on his work, he is also insulting him by implying that it wasn't Hooke's shoulders he stood on. Ouch!

"What happens to Hooke next?" asks Milton.

"The Royal Society publishes his book of drawings of objects seen through a microscope in 1665. It is called the *Micrographia* and makes him world famous. You must look it up. It's really beautiful as well as radically challenging to the big picture everyone had up to that point."

"So their big picture suddenly had to include the very, very small?"

"Exactly. People realized that there were more things in heaven and earth than could be seen with the naked eye. That is what Galileo showed when he pointed his telescope at the moon, and now Hooke will do the same for your flea."

"I forgive him for not liking cats then."

Hooke starts sneezing violently. "Dash it all, my eyes are watering. That cat must be about the place still." He picks up a paperweight, tossing it in preparation to throw it.

"We'd better go; we're holding up the advancement of science." Milton slips nimbly away into the time machine, holding the door ajar for Harriet. They leave Hooke grumbling and blowing his nose.

LONG TIME, NO SEA!

Robert Hooke wasn't the only outstanding instrument maker of the era. It's time to meet the father of time: John Harrison (1693–1776), clockmaker.

Before GPS, having an accurate clock was vital for seagoing. You needed two pieces of information to know where you were in the middle of an ocean: your north-south position (your latitude) and your east-west position (longitude). You could work out your latitude from the angle of a fixed star above the horizon. Finding longitude was more difficult but possible with an accurate clock.

Each hour of time is equal to 15° (360° divided by 24 hours). If you set your watch by noon at Greenwich and then observe the time at which the sun is at noon where you are, the time difference should tell you your longitude. The problem for ships' captains was that their timepieces were unreliable. A few minutes lost could be the difference between a clear passage and sailing onto rocks. Harrison helped solve that with his sea clocks, which kept the best time for timepieces in this era, and was continually improving on the design – or upgrading, as we now say.

What do you call a tense clock?

All wound up!

APPLE HARVEST

Harriet runs a comb over Milton's fur.

"There you go: no more fleas."

"Good. They are horrid things." Milton shakes himself.

"And they can be deadly. Hold still." She squeezes some flea repellant onto his neck. "That should keep them away."

"How are they deadly?"

"Cast your mind back. You've seen it before."

Milton remembers their earlier adventure in Paris. "The Black Death in medieval times?"

Harriet nods.

"We lost some good friends to that. Hang on a minute! I've just remembered my history lessons. It happens again, doesn't it?"

"That's right. That's why we're skipping over 1665 and 1666 in London. The plague never really goes away and returns again and again, but this is a particularly bad one."

Milton shivers. "But I haven't got it, have I?"

"No, Milton, the time machine protects us. And we have modern medicine now that can tackle it even if you did – partly thanks to the microscope."

JOHN GRAUNT: LEARNING TO COUNT

How do you know when the plague is coming?

Doctors knew it would be helpful to have an early warning system of disease so they could impose quarantine measures, but in a time before easy communication all they had to rely on were rumours and anecdotes.

There was a better way. One man in London pioneered a new method by taking a scientific approach to the problem. He wasn't someone you would think of as a scientist. By profession John Graunt was a musician, but numbers interested him. In 1662, he started looking at the Bills of Mortality in London (weekly lists of people who died) to see if he could detect the start of plague before it took hold. His work formed the basis for later census and statistical work on diseases, which is still vital in modern medicine and population planning.

What's interesting for our curious science quest is that the musician Graunt adopted a scientific method to solve an age-old problem. New ways of thinking were taking hold across society!

"What happened next," says Harriet, "is that there was a big fire in London and that killed a lot of the rats and fleas that carried the infection. But it killed a lot of people too and destroyed the London we've been visiting."

The time machine comes out of uncertainty and hovers over the fire in September 1666. All they can see of the centre of old London is the bright glow of orange flames and billows of black smoke.

"I don't want to go down there," says Milton, watching the people flee to the river.

"No, we'd better stay out of it. The Great Fire changes the lives of all the people we met at the Royal Society. Pepys writes about it – his account is the most famous one. Wren is asked to rebuild St Paul's and leaves his mark on modern London, and Hooke helps Wren with the mechanics needed for his designs, such as the great dome of the cathedral. Hooke also helps sort out what gets built on the scorched land after the fire. The damage is so bad, no one is sure where the old buildings and roads stood. Hooke moves swiftly to sort out disputes and help rebuild. He doesn't get enough credit for it, but he does a good job."

"OK, Hooke's a great man. I get it now. You don't have to like a person to see how important they are. So where are we going?"

"We are going to see an even greater thinker, so that must mean…?"

"I know this one!" Milton claps his paws. "Isaac Newton!"

 MEET THE SCIENTIST

SIR ISAAC NEWTON

- Lived: 1643–1727 AD
- Number of jobs: 7 (inventor, mathematician, physicist, theologian, warden of the Mint, president of the Royal Society, alchemist)
- Influence (out of 100): 100 (undoubtedly one of the most influential scientists)
- Right? (out of 20): 20 (laid the foundations of classical mechanics, made important discoveries in optics, and co-invented calculus in mathematics)
- Helpfully wrong? (out of 10): 6 (devoted years to alchemical research and numerology. Alchemy has the idea of a force acting at a distance; this may have helped him toward his ideas on gravity)

- Interesting fact: he had a teaching position at Trinity College, Cambridge, but wasn't the most gifted communicator. No student turned up for his second lecture. He continued dutifully delivering the course of lectures to an empty room.

Maybe my influence will act on my students from a distance?

"Correct. We're going to call in on him when he is a student at Cambridge, long before he becomes famous."

"Why not wait until he does something interesting?" grumbles Milton.

"He is always doing something interesting, and today he is going to the Stourbridge fair."

"A fair? A *proper* fair?" Milton is suspicious. "This isn't like your club that isn't a fun club, is it? I'm not letting you catch me out again."

"No, I mean a real fair with stalls and jugglers and acrobats and fortune tellers…"

"Excellent! I'm liking this adventure already."

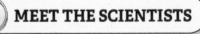

MEDICINE IN THE SPOTLIGHT

While Milton and Harriet head to Cambridge, let's drop in on two medical men: one from the start of the period and one from the end.

WILLIAM HARVEY

- Lived: 1578–1657 AD
- Number of jobs: 1 (doctor)
- Influence (out of 100): 60 (first to correctly identify the circulation of the blood)
- Right? (out of 20): 12 (he was hampered by not having access to a microscope, so couldn't see capillaries or the fine details of the circulatory system)
- Helpfully wrong? (out of 10): 0 (he was largely on the right track in anatomy)
- Interesting fact: not believing in witchcraft, he helped an alleged witch during the witch trials of the period. In 1632, he proved her "witch's familiar" (a toad) was an ordinary animal by dissecting it. She wasn't pleased, but at least she wasn't put on trial.

EDWARD JENNER

- Lived 1749–1823 AD
- Number of jobs: 2 (doctor and zoologist)
- Influence (out of 100): 95 (he pioneered vaccination and has arguably contributed to saving more lives than any other person. Wow!)
- Right? (out of 20): 18 (building on the work of others – including Turkish doctors and the traveller Lady Mary Wortley Montagu – he suggested that

exposure to a controlled amount of a disease would provide immunity. He tackled smallpox by giving people injections of cowpox; a less dangerous cow version of the disease)

- Helpfully wrong? (out of 10): not applicable, as he was right!
- Interesting fact: he was also interested in cuckoos. He was the first to observe that it was the baby cuckoo, not the adult, that tipped the other eggs and chicks out of the nest.

Harriet and Milton land in one of the grand quadrangles of Trinity College, Cambridge, in time to spot Newton heading out of the gate.

"Ho there, Master Newton! Remember you are on serving duty tonight!" calls one of the college porters.

Newton doesn't seem to hear as he is reading while walking. This makes it easy for Milton and Harriet to catch him up undetected.

"Head in the clouds, that one," complains the porter.

"Newton is enrolled as one of the poor students. He has to do chores to earn his place," whispers Harriet. "His mum doesn't like the idea of him going to college and wants him to stay home and manage the farm, so she keeps the money tight."

"He doesn't strike me as a natural farmer," muses Milton.

"At home, when they put him in charge of looking after the sheep, he promptly forgets them and sits under a tree whittling little mechanical toys. His mother is taking a long while to give up on her farming ambitions for him. She had asked him to manage the land, but discovered he was letting their servants do all the work while he studies."

"See! Early proof he's a clever boy, getting others to do his chores."

"He wasn't avoiding work; he just had a different kind to occupy his mind. He was working out the secrets of the universe!"

Cambridge at this time is a dirty place with narrow streets and low houses beyond the walls of the beautiful colleges. Milton and Harriet watch in surprise as Newton walks obliviously past at least three muggers and a street fight. Then a pickpocket goes for his purse, but Newton slaps his hand away.

"Maybe he isn't so blind after all," murmurs Milton, hopping over a pile of dung.

Harriet has to slowly make her way around it. "He's walking too fast for me now. He'll be there and back before I get to the fair!"

Suddenly, Newton turns and picks her off the ground. "Hmm, curious." He pops her into his pocket. "You shouldn't be here, should you?"

"Strictly speaking, no," admits Harriet. "Pretend we're not."

Newton passes a hand over his brow. "I've been studying too hard. I'm imagining you can speak." He smiles at the absurd idea. "Well, creature who isn't here, figment of my imagination, you are following me, aren't you?"

"Yes," Harriet admits.

"Why?"

"Because we want to go to the fair."

"We?"

"Me and my cat, Milton."

"A talking cat as well! I'm definitely doing too much studying," says Newton, rubbing his forehead.

They make swifter progress now that Newton is so obligingly carrying Harriet. They reach the fair, which is pitched on a muddy common. There are tents, wagons, and stalls – and a great number of people have come to enjoy themselves. He buys his two companions some honey cake and stops to admire the acrobats.

"Fascinating how they can perfectly judge the balancing point without ever wondering about the mathematics behind it. Ah!" Young Newton's eye has been caught by a stall selling glass pendants, which are twinkling in the sunshine. "Just what I was looking for."

The canny stallholder sees a prospective customer. She makes the pendants sway and sparkle. "Present for your sweetheart, young sir?"

"No, mistress. I need a prism for an investigation into the properties of light."

"He's very clever," adds Harriet, poking her head out of his pocket and addressing the stallholder. "Trust me, it's an honour to sell him one."

The woman gives a little shriek. "Oh, stars above! It talks! Here, take this, take this! Bargain price." She bundles a large glass prism into Newton's hand.

Newton passes over a handful of coins and retreats, very pleased with his purchase. He sits down on a bank of the river and revolves it in his fingers. "See how the light passes through the prism and emerges in many colours? The question is: has the glass changed the light somehow or is light itself made up of this rainbow? How can I test this?" He gets up. "Right, back to my rooms to try out a few ideas."

THE CURIOUS CASE OF THE COLOURS OF THE RAINBOW

How many colours are there in a rainbow?

Seven, you say.

Really? What if Harriet told you that Homer (the Greek storyteller) said there was one: purple? Xenophanes went for three and he was supported by Aristotle. In the Renaissance they thought four. Newton first counted five: red, yellow, green, blue, and violet. He later added orange and indigo because he thought seven a more elegant number as it matched notes in a musical scale.

In China today many people still count five. Baltic countries have a tradition of two: red and blue. Researchers have found that the number of colours seen depends on the culture and language of the person looking. Doesn't sound very scientific, does it?

The reason for the confusion is that the rainbow is a range, not separate colours, as one fades into another. You can slice the cake as you like!

Richard – Red
Of – Orange
York – Yellow
Gave – Green
Battle – Blue
In – Indigo
Vain – Violet

"Newton should've stopped at five!"

Harriet drops out of Newton's pocket when they return to the grassy spot where they left the time machine. Newton disappears into his room, still gazing at his prism.

"That's one of Newton's big themes," explains Harriet. "They call it optics, but it means the study of the properties of light."

Milton is licking his paws. He has snagged a toffee apple that someone dropped at the fair and eaten it on the way back. "And it all started with a visit to a fair?"

"That was one of the things that got him thinking, though he might well have already been wondering. He is curious about everything."

TRY THIS AT HOME:
CREATE YOUR OWN RAINBOW!

Would you like to follow in Newton's footsteps?

After leaving the fair, he went back to his room and thought up an experiment that would decide whether the prism added colours to the white light, or split it from white into many colours.

To make your rainbow, you don't need a prism – a shallow pan of water will do.

1. Half-fill a pan with water and place a small mirror on the bottom, not flat but wedged at an angle.

2. Place the pan in bright sunlight or shine a torch at the mirror.

3. Can you see a rainbow somewhere in your room? If not, hold a piece of paper over the pan and catch it! How many colours can you see?

You've made your rainbow, but it doesn't settle the question as to whether the mirror has added the colours or split the light. Newton worked out how to show that light was made up of a spectrum. He set up another prism, which captured the rainbow he had made and refocused it into a single beam. The light became white again. This proved nothing had been added to the beam of light.

Clever, huh?

TAKING THIS FURTHER

Scientists vary their experiments to see if a change will make any difference to the result. Can you think of a way you might do this? Here are two suggestions:

1. Increase the depth of water.

2. Add food dye to the water (don't forget to get permission for this and do it in a sensible location because food dye can stain fingers and clothes!).

What did you see?
What do you think this means?

What's this about an apple?

"I know what Newton's second big theme starts with," declares Milton proudly.

"Oh yes?"

"An apple." He holds up the core of his toffee apple. "Stop anyone in the street and they'll tell you that. Newton sat under a tree, got bonked on the head by an apple, and realized that the world had something called gravity."

Harriet passes him a cloth as he is getting sticky paw prints all over the controls. "Milton, that might never have happened. It's one of those stories that probably got added to and embellished over time."

Milton has a determined glint in his eye. "No, I want it to be true. Let's go and see."

Harriet shakes her head. "Prepare to be disappointed, then. We are heading back into the plague years of 1665 and 1666.

* ∴ ∴ ⁚* * ⁚*

"Newton leaves Cambridge to spend these years in relative safety on his family farm in Lincolnshire," Harriet continues.

Isaac, you should treat this subject with more gravity.

She lands the time machine in a field near Newton's farm at Woolsthorpe. In the distance, in an orchard, they can see their man sitting at a table taking tea.

A dog appears out of the bushes.

"There you are, Diamond!" says Harriet to the spaniel. "How is your master today?"

"Not another dog!" complains Milton.

"Why bring the scruff ball?" asks Diamond, miffed by Milton's tone.

"Milton is a scientific explorer and a friend. I'm sorry, but he's also very rude about dogs."

"Woof! As he's with you, Harriet, I'll forgive him. Once. After that…" Diamond gives Milton a challenging stare. Milton knows it is war if he says anything rude again. "As for my master, he has been very quiet all day. He is thinking and has let his tea get cold."

The three animals creep up behind Newton. He is murmuring about numbers and forces, scratching notes with a quill on ink-splattered paper. Milton looks up at the apples in the tree above Newton. They look as though they have a few weeks to go before they are ripe.

"See, it didn't happen!" whispers Harriet.

"We'll see about that!" mutters Milton. And before Harriet can stop him, he claws up the tree and sneaks out on the limb above Newton's head.

"Milton, get down here!" says Harriet. She is imagining all kinds of horrible consequences for the history of science if Milton does what she thinks he is about to do. "Don't risk it!"

Milton flicks his tail in cheeky refusal. He nudges a green apple. It doesn't move. He gives it a wallop and it plummets down to the ground. Milton sits back and blows on his claws, fully satisfied with himself.

But Newton doesn't notice.

What?!

"Milton!" Harriet tries again. "Timeline!"

But Milton just knows that he is part of the timeline. He's here, and it makes sense to him that someone gives Newton a hint. He starts to jump up and down on the branch. The leaves rustle and apples start to fall. Still Newton doesn't look up. Finally, one big red apple plops on Newton's head.

"Ouch!" Newton rubs the spot where it landed. He picks up the apple. "Hmm, I wonder…"

NEWTON'S APPLE OF AN IDEA

If matter draws matter it must be in proportion to its quantity… the apple draws the earth as the earth draws the apple.

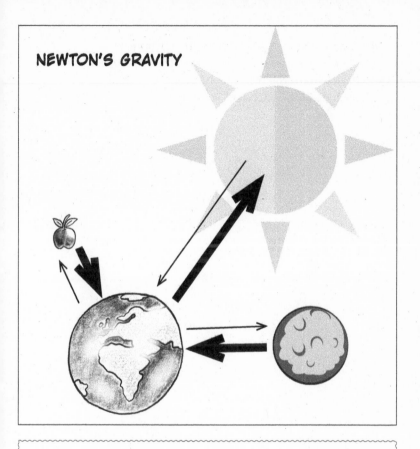

NEWTON'S GRAVITY

Matter is something that has a mass and takes up space, such as a gas, a liquid, or a solid.

Milton scrambles out of the tree and leaps down beside Harriet. His expression is exactly that of the cat that got the cream.

"There you are. Newton is on the path to being the greatest thanks to me!" he declares. "And the apple story is true!"

Harriet rolls her eyes. "Only because you made it so."

Diamond, however, is furious. "You threw apples at my master!"

Oh dear, thinks Milton. To every action, there is an equal and opposite reaction. That is also one of Newton's laws.

"Get out!" Diamond barks, then leaps at Milton, who makes a dash back toward the time machine.

"You'll thank me one day!" he protests, slamming the door on the angry dog.

NEWTON'S LAWS OF MOTION

One of the most exciting things about Newton as a scientific thinker was his ability to create general laws from what he saw. He was also able to describe them mathematically. He uncovered patterns in the universe that linked Galileo's terrestrial mechanics with Kepler's planetary laws. What happened on earth held true in the whole universe too. It's only much later in the twentieth century that any exceptions were discovered.[1]

Here are his revolutionary laws in simple language:

1. If an object is not moving it will not start moving by itself. If an object is moving it will not stop or change direction unless something pushes it.

2. Objects will move further and faster when they are pushed harder.

3. When an object is pushed in one direction there is always a resistance of the same size in the opposite direction.

---

1 Look out for book 6, and the weird and wonderful world of Einstein's Theory of Relativity.

THE GREAT DEBATE

"So Newton settles one of life's biggest mysteries: why do the planets move in an orbit around the sun? It's because of gravity," says Milton as he waves at Diamond through the porthole of the time machine. "Clever!"

"Stop teasing her. We're going to see lots more dogs, so you need to behave," says Harriet.

"Oh, do we have to?"

"Oh yes, because I want to take you to hear what is said in the great debate that rages for the rest of this period. By that I mean the end of the seventeenth and the whole of the eighteenth century. In many ways, it still rumbles on in our time. Newton's work was the spark that started it. There are two more dogs I want to introduce you to."

"Harriet! I did not sign up for this!" moans Milton. "I thought I would be meeting scientists, not dangerous creatures with teeth who want to chase me!"

"Too late now!" says Harriet gleefully. "I'm taking you to meet a French poodle."

"Oh goodie."

Harriet sets the destination for Paris. "And you said that Newton settled a mystery. That's true. But he also raised another one. Gravity is the force of attraction between physical bodies, like the earth to the sun and an apple to the centre of the earth. But what is it?"

"Didn't you just say?"

"I told you what it *does*; what we can measure and study. I haven't been able to explain what it *is* exactly, because scientists are still thinking about this. Albert Einstein, one of the people

76

we'll meet in the twentieth century, will say that gravity isn't even a force but a warping of space–time."

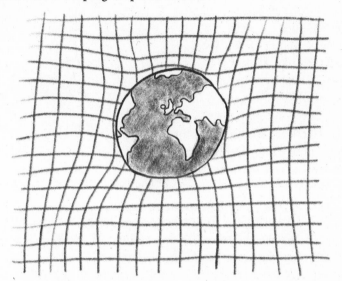

Milton collapses onto his woolly bed, paws in the air. "Freaky!"

"Completely. But for now, in Newton's time, a simple understanding of gravity is all we need. He is able to express it mathematically – that is a huge step forward – but his explanation of how things work also sets the cat among the pigeons."

Milton perks up. "That sounds like fun!"

Harriet opens the door and steps out into a library in Paris. "Welcome to the HQ of continental enlightenment!"

Milton frowns. "Those are long words. What do they mean?"

"Continental means mainland Europe. Enlightenment means when things become clear – the light bulb moment."

"Cool." He sniffs the books and licks one with golden letters. It tastes of dust.

Just as they are admiring the many books on the shelves, a poodle trots in.

"Bonjour, Olympe," says Harriet.

"Good day, Harriet. I see you brought the cat against my advice."

That silly poodle prances rather than walks, thinks Milton. "I don't want to be here, believe me."

"Do try to play nicely," says Harriet. "We are here for more important things than the old quarrel between cats and dogs."

"Indeed," agrees Olympe, jumping up so that her front paws rest on a desk. A big book lies open. "Come and admire the first volume of the *Encyclopedia*, made by my masters, Diderot and d'Alembert."

"The word 'encyclopedia' comes from the Greek language," Harriet whispers to Milton. "It means an all-round education. The Frenchmen are trying to gather the most up-to-date knowledge on everything that it is possible to know." She sighs in appreciation. This is exactly the kind of project she admires. "What an ambitious target! Other people are trying a similar thing, but theirs becomes the most famous in the world. It is the Wikipedia of its time."

Milton has cheered up considerably, having just discovered that one of the writers has left some cheese in his satchel. "Oh yes?" he says, pretending to show a polite interest as he hooks the Camembert rind with a back claw.

"Your cat's hopeless, isn't he?" says Olympe. "He doesn't understand how remarkable an achievement it is to have access to nearly all human knowledge in one place!"

Milton resists mentioning the Internet. "But what's it got to do with Newton?"

"You've come from the great Newton?" gasps Olympe. "My

masters and Monsieur Voltaire, to name but three of the leaders of my school of thought, say Newton is the most important thinker who ever lived."

"Why?" Milton is now genuinely interested and forgets about his attempt to steal the cheese.

Olympe turns to a page in the *Encyclopedia* to see a map of the solar system. "Before Newton we had a small, static picture of the world provided by religion. How do the planets move? Angels push them. Why do we exist? God created us. We continental materialists think we don't need the God hypothesis any more to explain how the world works. Newton provided a grand landscape picture of the heavens and earth controlled by scientific laws. They are our answers. Newton deserves a temple, not God."

"What's a materialist?" Milton asks.

"Someone who looks only to the physical world for answers," says Harriet. "Some thinkers go so far as to say that even our free will is an illusion. Everything has a physical cause."

Milton has met many scientists who think like this in the future, but hardly any in the past. "But Newton himself didn't think like that," he points out. "He thought God lay behind the order he found when he studied the universe."

The most beautiful system of the sun, planets, and comets could only proceed from the counsel and dominion of an intelligent and powerful being.

Signed
Isaac Newton

The poodle sniffs. "He wasn't as enlightened as us, then."

"And yet you want to build a temple to honour him?"

Harriet intervenes before the dog and cat begin to scrap. "We mustn't argue. People can look at the same facts and draw different conclusions. Science doesn't belong to one kind of picture-maker. Thank you for showing us the *Encyclopedia*, Olympe. I think your masters might be on to a good idea there!"

The poodle waves them off. "Tortoises are so much more polite than cats," she says in parting.

Watching out of the window just before the time machine leaves, Milton sees Olympe check that she isn't being observed before gulping down the cheese rind he had to abandon.

"I bet I'll still get the blame," he thinks gloomily.

Harriet rummages in a cupboard and comes back with some of their own cheese for Milton.

"Here, have this. Stealing is never a good idea and I'm glad you didn't eat that rind. Oddly enough, theft was one of Newton's greatest fears – though in his case, he was thinking about the stealing of ideas. It made him very secretive and difficult to work with. I'll show you by taking you to the next stop in the great debate."

Milton isn't sure he deserves the cheese. "Will there be a dog?"

"Oh yes," says Harriet cheerfully. "A German shepherd."

Milton jumps into the cupboard and closes the door. "I'm not coming out."

"Oh, Milton. He really is a very friendly creature!"

"It's all right for you to say that!"

Harriet lands the time machine in Leipzig, Germany. "Aren't you going to give him a chance?" she calls to Milton.

"No!" Milton's voice sounds very muffled as he has squeezed in with all their luggage and stores.

With a sigh, Harriet opens the door to the outside. Wilhelm, the German shepherd, is waiting for her, his tail wagging.

"Isn't this just the best of the best of all possible worlds?" he barks happily.

Harriet looks up at the sky. It is a rainy day in 1715 and the streets of Leipzig are very muddy. "I can imagine better."

"Oh no, but you can't!" Wilhelm is running in circles now. "It was created by God, and he can only create that which is perfect, so therefore it must be the best of the best!"

"What about earthquakes, illness, and war?" calls Milton from inside his cupboard.

"You have a talking cupboard. How quaint!" barks Wilhelm.

Harriet bangs on the cupboard door. "This is ridiculous, Milton!"

Milton pokes his head out. "Do you promise not to chase me?"

Wilhelm pants, looking extraordinary pleased with everything. "Of course, because this is the best of all possible days."

"But what if your best involves an exciting cat chase? That's good for you and bad for me," Milton points out.

Wilhelm's tail stops wagging. "Oh." Then his tail starts again. "I remember the answer to that: my master says that such bad things are the result of God giving us free will. If I choose not to chase you, then we will both be happy."

Milton slides out of the cupboard. "Pleased to meet you, then. But is your master a scientist? He sounds more like a philosopher."

"Come see my city." Wilhelm starts walking and wagging his tail at the same time. Quite an achievement, thinks Milton. "My master, Mr Gottfried Wilhelm Leibniz, is both a philosopher and a scientific thinker. He is most famous, though, as a mathematician.

He has come up with this fabulous method for calculating the area under a curve on a graph. He calls it calculus."

They stop outside a shop where two women are arguing over a pair of boots that have just gone on sale.

"That's a little like my master and Sir Isaac Newton arguing over who was first. They both came up with a similar set of mathematical tools to solve the problem of calculating a curve. I don't believe Newton published his. He was worried his ideas would be stolen, and just wrote private letters about it. My master went into print. When Newton saw my master was thinking along the same lines he was suspicious that Leibniz must have seen his work somehow."

"I think Newton was reluctant to believe that anyone else might be as bright as him and come up with it on their own," agrees Harriet. "But I think, Wilhelm, that history will decide they were both very clever, but your master's way of doing it is a little easier to work with. Future generations will make good use of it."

Wilhelm woofs with laughter as the shopkeeper offers a single boot to each woman as a compromise. They stalk off, leaving the boots for another lucky customer. "Oh, isn't this fun?!"

BAYES' THEOREM: WHAT'S THE PROBABILITY OF THAT?

This stage of our curious science quest is full of interesting mathematical thinkers, not just Newton and Leibniz. One of these, Thomas Bayes, was a mathematician and church minister who lived in London and Kent (1701–1761). He is most famous for the theorem that is named after him, which is still used today in machine learning. The theorem looks at the question of how to calculate the probability of something when you know information about prior conditions related to that event.

Confused? It's easier to see it in practice.

Here's a simple example. You put six red and six black balls in a bag. You draw out two red. The conditions have changed. What is the probability now that you'll pull out another red?

This same approach can help with much more complicated situations, and is the basis for modern machines learning on the job. Next time you look in the spam folder of your emails, you'll see messages sent there by machines that have learned to filter certain information thanks to Bayes's theorem!

The German shepherd pauses for a drink at a public fountain, barks merrily at the pigeons, then continues.

"That is not the only thing my master and Newton argue about. My master is exchanging letters with a friend of Newton's, knowing the great man will see them and suggest the replies. My master is saying that Newton has some things wrong about his big picture. He agrees that God is behind the universe but thinks that Newton's explanation leaves a weakness. By coming up with more and more mechanical explanations for how the universe works, he is closing the gaps in which God is traditionally given as the answer. If this goes too far there will be no more gaps – a closed system and no God."

"That's what the poodle thinks," says Milton. "God has vanished from her model. It's a powerful argument."

"But painting a picture of the universe where God only fits in gaps is the wrong way to think about things," says Wilhelm. "Because, of course, as science finds out more answers the areas of uncertainty change or vanish entirely."

"So how else can we think about these things?" wonders Milton.

He is so interested in this debate that he has forgotten to be scared of the big German shepherd dog. He runs alongside him as they move into the shadow of the clock in the market square.

"There are three main choices in this debate," says Wilhelm. "You have scientists in Britain saying there is a divine order. God creates the universe like a clockmaker, sets it running, and steps back. That leads to the God-of-the-gaps explanation as they say he has come in and fiddled with the mechanism if they don't understand how it works. Then you have my friend Olympe's materialists getting rid of the clockmaker altogether and saying that the universe works without a creator. My master wants a third way that doesn't fall into either camp."

"So what's left?" asks Milton.

"To answer that we have to return to France and our other friend, Marie the gun dog," says Harriet. "Her master, Blaise Pascal, has a helpful third view on this subject. Thank you, Wilhelm, for keeping us company!"

Wilhelm barks happily. "This has been the best day ever!"

"So what do you think of dogs now?" Harriet asks Milton once they are travelling again.

"If they were all like Wilhelm, maybe I'd actually be friends with one." Milton is very impressed by Wilhelm's parting gift of a German sausage. "I haven't tasted anything as good as this since our visit to the first printing press!"

Harriet huffs. "Are you going to continue to see our trip around the most curious moments in science as a tour of the world's best foods?"

"Probably," admits Milton happily.

The time machine lands in the French city of Rouen and Milton peers out of the window. It is a bustling place with a superb cathedral.

"So when are we, Harriet?"

"It's a few years after the barometer experiment. I'm afraid Pascal is not enjoying very good health. He is working on a book that will be published after his death – aged only thirty-nine – in 1662. It is called *Pensées* – or *Thoughts* – and remains very famous today."

Marie has been looking out for them. She bounds up, still as excited as ever.

"Hello, my friends! Come and meet my master!" She takes them to a house in the city. Jumping over the garden fence, or in Harriet's case climbing carefully, they look in through a ground-floor window. Pascal is bent over an odd brass box with six wheels on the top.

"What's that?" asks Harriet. "It looks complicated!"

"My master's calculating machine. He made it when he was only nineteen to help his father in his job as a tax collector. It can add and subtract long strings of numbers, accurately keeping tally through its clever carry-over mechanism. He keeps on improving it, so maybe one day everyone will have a machine like this to do sums."

"Maybe," says Milton with a smile.

"He's really good at mathematics. Have you seen his triangle?" asks Marie.

"No," says Milton.

Marie scratches it out on the ground with her paw. "You can have a go filling it out."

PASCAL'S TRIANGLE

To build the triangle, start with "1" at the top, then continue placing the numbers below it in a triangular pattern. Each number is the total of the numbers directly above it added together.

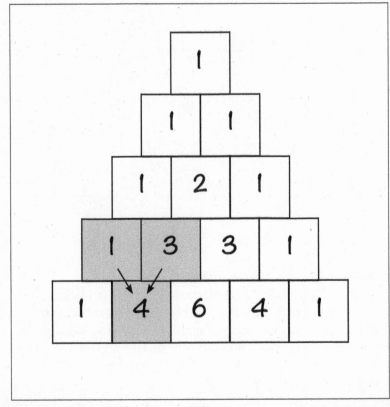

PATTERNS WITHIN THE TRIANGLE

Diagonals
- The first diagonal is, of course, just 1s.
- The next diagonal has the counting numbers (1, 2, 3, etc).
- The third diagonal has the triangular numbers.

There are lots of other interesting patterns in the triangle for you to explore.[2]

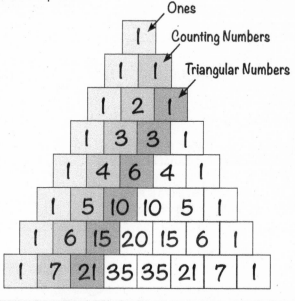

"Oh, I like that," purrs Milton. "I can see that this is going to entertain me for ages! Look what it does if you keep going!"

"My master also worked with another famous mathematician, Pierre de Fermat, on probability theory," says Marie proudly. "He really does have the most curious mind for numbers."

"Ah, there you are, Marie!" Pascal walks slowly over to the

window and rubs her head. "Found some friends, have you? I've been having some very intriguing thoughts inspired by my reading today – thoughts about the microscope and the telescope. Do you know what I realized? That every area of science is infinite in how far we can go in our research! It really is a very exciting age of progress we are living through!"

"What other thoughts do you have, sir?" asks Harriet.

"Good gracious, a talking tortoise. Now that *is* something!" Pascal peers at her. "I must have fallen asleep after lunch and still be dreaming."

"Or maybe we are time-travelling creatures from the future," she suggests.

"Hmm, now what would the probability of that be?"

THOUGHT FOR THE DAY

We know there is an infinite number, but do not know what it is... So we can clearly understand that there is a God without knowing who he is.

It is the heart that feels God, not reason... The heart has its reasons, which reason itself does not know.

"We've just come from Leipzig and we were talking about the God-of-the-gaps argument," says Milton.

"Now the cat talks! Next you'll be telling me my dog does too."

Marie tries to look like a dog who wouldn't dream of doing anything so odd as to talk. She fails. Pascal gives her a suspicious look.

Harriet nudges him.

"Well now, where were we? God of the gaps, eh? That is as wrong as the idea that the French thinkers have that everything has a material cause and there is no God. Both schools of thought burn with desire to find a firm foundation, an unchanging solid base on which to build a tower that rises forever. The problem with that is the foundation so often splits as science moves on and everything you've built on it crumbles. We are left gazing up at the eternal silence of the infinite spaces." He gazes up at the sky.

"A scientific thinker who is also a poet!" says Milton to Harriet. "I like him!"

"Not that I dismiss the power of reason," Pascal continues. "We humans are but a frail reed blowing in the wind, but we are a thinking reed and our task is to think well."

"So you believe there is a God, but not a God of the gaps?"

"Oh yes, but I seek him in here," Pascal points to his heart, "not in nature out there."

"How can you be sure you've found him?" asks Milton. "What is your evidence?"

"What kind of evidence would there be of this? My heart feels it is so, but also I believe because it is a good wager to take. Think about it like this: you bet with your life on whether there is a God or not. I think that the most rational choice is to live as though God exists, and seek to believe in him.'

"Why do that?" asks Milton.

Pascal smiles. "Well, if God does not exist I will have only a small loss in life from living it by religious rules. For example, maybe I won't eat certain foods or swear, and I'll go to church needlessly. However, if God *does* exist, I stand to receive infinite gains in heaven and avoid infinite losses by being separated from God as an unbeliever."

"I see," says Milton. "And I suppose if he doesn't you'll never know the outcome of the wager anyway."

"Excellently put, dear cat. Now, how about some milk?"

SHOCKING SCIENCE: ELECTRICITY

While our time travellers take a well-deserved rest, let's find out what is happening in a really important area of scientific curiosity. The eighteenth century was a time when scientists began to make big steps forward in the investigation of electricity. Until then, electricity had been a poorly understood phenomenon, but three thinkers in particular helped push knowledge forward.

1 The first is a German pastor called Ewald Georg von Kleist (1700–1748). He invented a jar that could store static electricity and sent it to Leyden University for further investigation. A Dutch graduate student (Pieter van Musschenbroek) tidied up the research, so he also has a claim to have invented it. That's why we now know it as a Leyden jar.

In this early form it was a water-filled jar with a metal spike through the stopper that was long enough to touch the water.

2 The second thinker is Benjamin Franklin (1705–1790). As well as his day job of founding the United States of America, he made time to investigate the nature of electricity, in particular lightning. He is famous for the flying-the-kite-in-a-thunderstorm experiment of 1752 – definitely NOT one to try at home. Franklin knew to stand on an insulator and keep dry to avoid a shock, but other scientists weren't so lucky!

Here is a safe experiment you can try.

TRY THIS AT HOME: MAKE YOUR OWN LIGHTNING ROD

Lightning is the same type of force as static electricity – the kind you can get when touching another person or pulling a woolly jumper over your head.

You will need: a plastic fork, tin foil, a balloon

1. Wrap the tinfoil around a plastic fork.

2. Inflate the balloon.

3. Put on a rubber glove and rub a balloon against your hair or woolly clothes.

4. Place the fork against the balloon and touch the foil with your other hand.

Did you see the spark? It will help to do this in a darkened room.

You could vary the experiment by rubbing the balloon against different materials to see which produce static and which don't.

3 The third of our electrical geniuses is Alessandro Volta (1745–1827). He was an Italian chemist and physicist who, in 1799, invented the first chemical battery called the voltaic pile by alternating electrodes of zinc and copper in a bath of diluted sulfuric acid or brine. This chemically produced electricity debunked the theory that only living things generated electricity.

An electrode lets electricity enter or leave an object, substance, or area. This is called a conductor, allowing the flow of energy around a circuit.

That idea was sponsored by another Italian, Luigi Galvani, who discovered what he called "animal electricity" when he connected two metal rods to frogs' legs and saw them twitch (he gave us the word "galvanize", which means "to leap into action"). Galvani's experiment led to people thinking that electricity was in some way the source of life.

The most striking use of this idea came from an eighteen-year-old girl named Mary Shelley in a book called *Frankenstein*, first published in 1818. In her story, the creature is brought to life by an electrical charge and goes on the rampage when his scientist creator rejects him. Her novel has become an image of a scientific experiment that has run out of control!

REACH FOR THE STARS

Back inside the time machine, Milton is lying on his woolly bed, thinking. Harriet begins to worry about him as he's not normally so quiet. It's been hours since he even mentioned food.

"What's the matter, Milton?" she asks.

"I was wondering what my big picture of the universe is now that I've heard about the great debate. I'm not sure how I will come to a decision, as everyone makes good points. Do I look for the deep patterns in nature and think there's a God behind it? Do I decide the universe can work very well without a creator at all? Or do I take Pascal's advice and look to my heart to decide?"

Harriet ponders the question. It is perhaps the biggest one there is, so she wants to give him a good answer. "Everyone has to decide this for themselves. But one thing to consider is where we started, back when we were outside the Cavendish Laboratory in Cambridge. We agreed that there were big, ultimate questions like 'Is there a God?' and penultimate ones like 'How do the planets revolve around the sun?' Scientific answers might help us with the big questions, but there are other places to look. Not all knowledge is scientific."

"Where do I go, then?" asks Milton.

"There are lots of places. If I'm wondering about God I'd start with the key religious books, such as the Bible. I'd also ask the opinions of people who have thought about these things – philosophers and theologians – or I'd read about or talk to those who have been especially wise and loving in how they lived their lives. I'd be interested in their opinions as they seem to be the best witnesses. Art, poetry, music, and songs – they can teach us a lot too. I'd also ask what my heart believes."

Milton ties knots in the blue wool with his back paws. "I thought Pascal sounded like a poet."

Harriet smiles. "Yes, scientists can be poetic as well."

"So where are we going next?"

"I'm glad you asked," says Harriet. "I thought we'd pay a call on a cracking brother-and-sister team who expanded even further our idea of the universe."

Milton shakes himself free from the tangle of wool. "Hit the button, Harriet! I'm ready for my next adventure!"

ALCHEMY IS DEAD: LONG LIVE CHEMISTRY!

While Harriet and Milton spin off to their next stop, let's have a look at what is going on at this time in chemistry. During the seventeenth century our time travellers were still meeting serious scientists who were also fans of alchemy, such as Newton and Boyle. By the end of the eighteenth century there were none left.

What changed?

It's time to meet two scientists who helped make chemistry professional and put an end to alchemy as a serious subject.

 MEET THE SCIENTISTS

JOSEPH PRIESTLEY

- Lived: 1733–1804 AD
- Number of jobs: 5 (minister of religion, educator, chemist, theologian, and political writer)
- Influence (out of 100): 40 (one of the first chemists to isolate oxygen, created soda water, and wrote about electricity)
- Right? (out of 20): 10 (he isolated a number of gases but stuck to the theory of phlogiston – that air contains a fire-like substance, which is released during combustion). This isolated him from other chemists)
- Helpfully wrong? (out of 10): 6 (though wrong, the phlogiston theory led him to become the first to make a correct link between blood and air in respiration)
- Interesting fact: he was chased out of Birmingham in 1791 for his religious and political views in support of the French Revolution. The event became known as the Priestley Riots. His laboratory and library were destroyed by the mob.

That's taking phlogiston research too far!

ANTOINE-LAURENT DE LAVOISIER

- Lived: 1743–1794 AD
- Number of jobs: 2 (chemist and administrator)
- Influence (out of 100): 88 (established chemistry in its modern form, discovered a number of elements, and reformed the naming system for elements)
- Right? (out of 20): 18 (made many key discoveries, including isolating oxygen and hydrogen. He established that although matter might change in appearance its mass remains the same)
- Helpfully wrong? (out of 10): 0 (he seems to have been on the right track in chemistry)
- Interesting fact: he died on the guillotine as a victim of the French Revolution. This wasn't for his scientific work, but for his role in administering taxes and controlling the sale of tobacco.

Why are chemists great for solving problems?

They have all the solutions!

Getting into Bath!

The time machine lands in Bath, England, in 1779. Milton is surprised to see Harriet checking her reflection before they head out to meet their next scientific explorer.

"Harriet, what are you doing?" Milton asks.

"Bath is the smartest city in the world at this time. People come here from all over Georgian England to take the water cure in the Grand Pump Room and dance the night away at the Assembly Rooms. I just want to make sure I look good enough to go out in public."

"You've never worried about that before." Milton wonders what is going on, then remembers they are getting close to Harriet's own time, so she might be more worried about meeting people she knows.

"Milton, I think your fur needs a little brush." Harriet approaches him with a comb.

"Leave it out, Harriet. I'll just give myself a quick lick. I'm sure I'm quite good enough for 1779."

Harriet gives a sniff and opens the door. She has put on what Milton thinks is a quite ridiculous bonnet, but he doesn't want to hurt her feelings.

They step out onto a busy street lit by torches. As Harriet said, the fashionable people are flocking to the Assembly Rooms. The ladies are in long silk dresses, the men in beautifully cut suits. Milton gives his scruffy coat a sly lick. Maybe Harriet has a point, he realizes. He does need a wash and a brush.

Music pours out through the open door. Inside, people are dancing. It looks so pretty, Milton is quite mesmerized. It reminds him of the orbits of the planets as ladies and gentlemen revolve around each other.

"Our scientist came here from Germany because he was first a musician," explains Harriet. "There are lots of jobs here for high-class performers. He plays many instruments and composes music before he becomes a full-time astronomer. His house is just down here on New King Street. He is about to meet someone who recognizes the brilliance of the young amateur stargazer."

They find William Herschel setting up his telescope on the street to look at the moon. A gentleman approaches, his silver-topped cane clicking on the cobbles.

"Good evening. Good viewing?" asks the stranger.

"Excellent, sir," says Herschel, adjusting the focus.

"May I?"

"Be my guest."

The stranger bends toward the eyepiece. "Good lord! This is the best telescope I've ever looked through. Where did you get it?"

"I made it myself."

"Made it? Are you a scientific instrument maker?"

William laughs. "No, I'm the organist at the Octagon Chapel."

"Young man, you are wasted on music. I predict a great future for you as an astronomer."

The men part on friendly terms, promising to meet up again soon.

"That other man is Dr William Watson," whispers Harriet. "He introduces the young musician to leading astronomers. This chance meeting turns our William from music to science.

He rapidly impresses his fellow stargazers and is made the King's Astronomer in 1782. He moves to a village called Datchet with his sister Caroline so he can have more room for the big telescopes he is constructing. Let's go and see – they really are impressive."

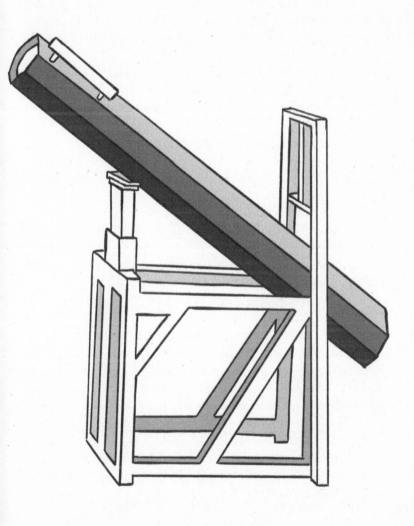

It's just a short hop in the time machine to 1783. They arrive on a cold winter's night and enter the astronomer's house by climbing over the back wall. William and Caroline Herschel are in the garden, dressed for a night of watching the stars. Caroline is at a desk taking notes. William, however, is up in the air, balanced on a cross-beam that holds his six-metre (twenty-foot) telescope.

"Did you get that, Lina?" He calls down.

"The ink is frozen on my quill, William! We'll have to stop! And it's too windy."

Harriet offers Milton the end of her scarf, so they sit and watch wrapped up warmly – unlike the Herschels.

"Careful now!" calls Caroline as William begins the dangerous climb down.

William's foot slips. As he catches himself on the wooden structure it snaps and the whole frame comes tumbling down. Milton drags Harriet clear of it by tugging on the scarf just in time.

"Is he all right?" asks Milton.

"William? William?!" calls Caroline, clambering over the wreckage to reach her brother.

"I'm unhurt, Lina. You'd better get help," says William from within the debris of his telescope.

As no more science is going to be done that day, Harriet and Milton head back inside the time machine.

"That just shows how dangerous science can be if you don't take care with safety measures," says Harriet. "I'm afraid the Herschels are a little accident-prone. Poor Caroline gets her knee impaled on a hook just a month after this! It's a serious wound and troubles her for years. However, I'd like to call back on a more peaceful night around this time because something significant is about to happen."

They emerge in the garden a second time. Gone are the howling winds and icy conditions. It looks like Caroline and William are having a private party.

"I have made you something, Lina," says William. He hands his sister a long parcel.

"Oh, good – I love presents," says Milton. "What's he giving her?"

"Watch," whispers Harriet. "I really like this moment in the history of science."

Caroline, a tiny lady, opens the big parcel, which is taller than her. "Oh, William! My own telescope!"

"You've helped me so much with my work I thought it was time you had your own so you could make your own discoveries. Let's set it up and find out what we can see tonight," says her brother.

The brother and sister erect the telescope next to William's bigger instrument.

"He is particularly skilled at making the lenses needed for these telescopes," says Harriet. "Caroline has helped him for years by taking down the position of stars as he gazes at the sky. It would ruin his eyesight to have to keep breaking away from the darkness to write notes in candlelight, so they have developed a clever collaboration to make the most of their time."

Caroline is now peering through the eyepiece. "Oh, I can see your new planet, Georgium Sidus!"

"That was the name William gave the planet he discovered in 1781, in honour of King George III. The name didn't stick and we now know it as Uranus," explains Harriet.

"And we'll be able to look for more double stars and comets together," says William. "It's a perfect night, with next to no clouds. Let's start marking their positions."

They work in silence for a while.

"Isn't it marvellous, Lina?" says William to his sister.

"It is indeed. But some people are saying that by expanding our knowledge of the universe so far and so fast we might undermine people's faith. They might get the impression we are leaving the ideas of religion behind."

"I don't find that, Lina. The more we know the bigger our picture becomes. I think that by investigating the magnificent structure of the universe we are taking forward the glory of the benevolent, intelligent, and superintending deity!" exclaims William.

As the two astronomers settle down for a long night of stargazing, Harriet and Milton creep away.

"It's lovely to see a brother helping his sister get into science," says Harriet. "People often ask why there aren't more female scientists, and this shows one reason. Caroline wasn't given the same encouragement and educational chances as her brothers until she came to live with William. In fact, she was very unhappy and horribly bullied by her older brother back in Hanover, Germany. She was working like a servant and certainly had no time to study. After she moved to be with William he saw how bright and interested she was, so he gave her the same tools he had himself. Many other girls who liked science weren't as fortunate."

"Does Caroline make her own discoveries?" asks Milton.

"Oh yes. She discovers eight comets, one of which is named after her. She lives to be ninety-seven and receives many awards – which was almost unheard of for a woman at this time – including the Gold Medal of the Royal Astronomical Society in 1828.

For a star stargazer!

Clap, Clap Clap!

"Her brother goes on to make bigger and bigger telescopes – even one that was twelve metres (forty feet) long. He makes lots of exciting discoveries, including several about the motions of binary stars, the rings of Saturn, and the dimensions of the Milky Way.

"And together the brother and sister team find 466 new nebulae. That's quite a record for the time."

A nebula is a cloud of gas and dust in outer space. New stars are formed in nebulae.

Milton circles and curls up on his woolly bed. "We're a kind of scientific partnership, aren't we?"

"That's right, Milton."

"And travelling together, we get bigger and bigger ideas about what our picture of the universe is like."

"Exactly. And as for the ultimate questions, I think William is right. While we're hunting for secrets of the universe, what matters is not whether God is big enough to survive, but whether our idea of God is big enough. William was able to look further into the skies than anyone and reconcile what he saw with his faith. The really big challenge to people's ideas about God and science didn't come from the stars but from something much closer to home."

"What challenge?"

"A finch's beak, among other things."

Milton licks his lips.

"Milton, the finches are not for chasing. We are hunting ideas, not birds!" warns Harriet.

Milton gives up on that little daydream of a happy bird-chasing adventure. "So we have another curious quest to go on?"

"Oh yes, but this one is with my master, Charles Darwin. We are off on a Victorian voyage of discovery. Are you ready?"

"Yes indeed! I'll dig out my sea voyage gear." Milton rummages around in the cupboard and comes out with a rubber ring. He can't swim. "But what happens if we meet you at an earlier stage? That would be a huge time-travel paradox!"

"Well, we'll just have to see, won't we?" says Harriet. "Buckle up! We're off to the nineteenth century and the voyage of a ship called *The Beagle*!"

Where to go to find out more

Harriet and Milton only flew past the Great Fire of London. If you want to find out more, try this game and help two children escape the fire: **http://www.fireoflondon.org.uk/game**

Newton's age is a great time to get experimenting. Many of the 'try this at home' experiments suggested in this book are thanks to Professor Berry Billingsley and Dr Finley Lawson at Learning about Science and Religion, Canterbury Christ Church University. You can find out more about their work and discover more experiments on their website: **http://lasarcentre.com**

Want to find out more about Pascal's curious maths? Then go to **https://www.mathsisfun.com/pascals-triangle.html**

Excited by Giambattista's spy egg? There are lots more simple spy experiments to try on **https://gb.education.com/slideshow/spy-science-slideshow/forensice-science-csi-kit/**

Answers
How many times did you spot the Curiosity Bug? The answer is 20.

Meet the authors

Julia Golding is a multi-award-winning children's novelist, including the *Cat Royal Series*, the *Companions Quartet*, and *The Curious Crime*. Having given up on science at sixteen, she became interested again when she realized just how inspiring science can be. It really does tell the best stories! This is her first experiment with non-fiction but hopefully her collaborators, Roger and Andrew, will prevent any laboratory accidents.

Andrew Briggs is the professor of nanomaterials at the University of Oxford. Nanomaterials just means small stuff. In his laboratory he studies problems like how electricity flows through a single molecule (you can't get stuff much smaller than a single molecule). He is also curious about big questions. He flies aeroplanes, but he has never been in a time travel machine like the one that Harriet and Milton use – yet!

Roger Wagner is an artist who paints power stations and angels (among other things) and has work in collections around the world. He didn't do the drawings for these books, but like Milton and Harriet he wanted to find out how the 'big picture' thinking of artists was connected to what scientists do. When he met Andrew Briggs the two of them set out on a journey to answer that question. Their journey (which they described in a book called *The Penultimate Curiosity*) was almost (but not quite) as exciting as Milton and Harriet's.

Harriet and Milton continue
their quest in

VICTORIAN
VOYAGES

– coming soon!